Be

A 30 Day Book of Prayers

Dawn Hill

Introduction

Another prayer book, those were my initial thoughts as I decided to release this book.

What would make it so different from the hundreds of others already on the market, why should someone buy my book?

These are the thoughts that I dealt with as I wrestled with God for a long while on releasing a book of prayers, after all I have launched multiple things over the last five years and gotten pretty much nowhere. Have you ever had those same self-defeating thoughts? I hope I am not the only one lol.

It seems many times the assignments God gives us are simple and profound but we have to make it complicated by second guessing ourselves. I am so glad God doesn't do this can you imagine God questioning if He was sure He wanted to create the earth? That would have been quite a mess, light on, light off, light on. As he questioned himself.

Ok, maybe that's a stretch but if we are made in his image why is it so hard for us to just accept what He tells us to do? Oh yeah that free will thing, that's fun right? Ok, all joking aside I am so happy to release my prayer book. I am sure it will be a series of books released every quarter to help spur your own prayer life and offer encouragement and hope. I mean if I can talk to God so can you, and isn't that what prayer is?

So in these pages you will see my real and raw prayers, many times it's my repenting and coming to the realization I don't know squat and have yet again run off and done it on my own. This particular set of prayers was born out of a really intense season of stripping. Those seasons where you know it's good for you but man it's not easy or fun to walk thru. It's in these moments at least for me that I find God really presses me for more and to become more of what He designed me to be, a pure hearted person with love for all.

That sounds so saintly, but the reality is I am strong and passionate human being made in a form of a woman who truly desires to live her best life and many times thinks she knows best, who said fathers knows best anyway, moms truly run the world. Look as far back as Mary helping push Jesus out of his comfort zone to turn the water into wine, see we really do know best.

I mean no disrespect to men or fathers on earth truly they have a role I mean mine personally wasn't present so I had to rely on God to be that for me for a very long time, trouble is I saw him with hurt and wounded eyes so I truly didn't trust God even, because I saw him thru the lens of my earthly father instead of the amazing unable to lie Creator that God is .

So when I say this season was intense I mean it's been the second most intense season of pruning I can remember in my life with God. I literally had been stripped down to bare bones so to speak. No cash, back down to a one car family, and our home in a messy estate situation that was headed quickly for foreclosure. Oh and to top it all off I had created most of this mess myself running ahead of God and trusting myself instead of seeking Him first. Yep that's the truth and it's not easy to confess.

So it's my prayer as you read these pages and truly take time to find your own experiences that may parallel these, that you will find more of God and true peace, love, and a desire to trust Him even more! I hope my words fall to the ground but His are hidden deep in your heart.

Thank you for taking time and money to sow into this book for yourself and for me and mine. I don't know exactly where this all goes or what my future holds but I truly know the One who holds my future and yours and He is awesome.

Blessings, read on, meditate on His word and maybe even find your relationship with God empowered and brightened by this journey thru prayer!

Much love,

Dawn

Day 1

Father,

Today I ask for you to heal our hearts. We have suffered many trials and traumas and it's so hard to truly let it go. With you all things are possible so we know if can fully release it to you, you can heal us.

We trust you Father and we are so grateful for grace and your love for us. Today just wrap Your arms around us so we can feel your presence and know beyond a shadow of doubt that if we forgive and let it go you will indeed comfort and heal

In Jesus name

Amen

Jeremiah 33:6

6 Behold, I will bring it health and cure, and I will cure them, and will reveal unto them the abundance of peace and truth.

Notes

Notes

Day 2

Abba,

Today we need our daddy. We are facing some giants in the land. All we have is a stone and a slingshot and he comes against us with greater weapons. It seems impossible.

Your word Abba says nothing is impossible to him who believes and all things are possible with Christ. So today Abba we take shelter under your mighty wing and we say help us, Daddy.

As we step out into the battlefield of life with what feels like no good weapons, we remember that we don't fight against flesh and blood and we also remember you fight for us, with us, and in us so we drawback our slingshot with the stone and we launch into today knowing the giants will fall!

In Jesus mighty name

Amen and amen

1 Samuel 17:49

49 Reaching into his bag and taking out a stone, he slung it and struck the Philistine on the forehead. The stone sank into his forehead, and he fell face down on the ground.

Notes

Notes

Day 3

Dear Lord

Today I would like to know exactly how it's all going to work out. I would like an exact schedule of events please, lol. I know that would not be faith if I knew exactly how it works out, I also know your thoughts are higher than mine.

I do trust you and I absolutely know you will work it out for my good and your glory however my flesh wants answers.

I love you Lord I work every day to surrender to the process of life that leads me to and thru the refiner's fire and that process is not easy but oh I am so blessed on the other side of it.

So, I say thank you and forgive me for my impatience and thank you for loving me while I grow to become the woman you made me to be!

I love you Lord,

In Jesus name I pray

Amen

Hebrews 11:1

11 Now faith is confidence in what we hope for) and assurance about what we do not see

Notes

Notes

Day 4

Father God,

Today I want to ask forgiveness for us as a people in the USA. We have put people in an idol place and looked to them to save us instead of our amazing God in heaven.

Lord it's so easy as people to look to other people to be our savior I think because we can tangibly see them. It's also easy to blame people for the state of our nations when in fact we have much blame to bear on this fact as well.

Lord, you gave us instructions in your word that help us to stay out of trouble yet we forget or ignore those instructions. We don't always do it on purpose but none the less we are guilty of idolatry. From looking to my own husband to solve my problems when we have a crisis instead of simply seeking your face at all times, I ask forgiveness for myself and stand in the gap for our nation.

Lord, please heal our land and release your fire over us and be with us in the shaking as you never leave us or forsake us. Help us to realize the quicker we come to you the faster we will see that healing!

In Jesus name

Amen

2 Chronicles 7:14

14 If my people, which are called by my name, shall humble themselves, and pray, and seek my face, and turn from their wicked ways; then will I hear from heaven, and will forgive their sin, and will heal their land.

Notes

Notes

Day 5

Dear God,

Today I pray for the dreamers and the dreams. Today I ask that you bring life to those who have lost their ability to believe or dream.

I pray for those who no longer believe it's going to happen. I pray they will look beyond what their natural eyes can see and the current circumstances and just find that sliver of hope to believe yet one more time.

I pray for 🔥 to be ignited deep in their soul that nothing is impossible with you God! I pray they can take their eyes off the world and simply put their eyes on your first and watch as everything is indeed added unto them just as you said!

Thank you for dreams thank you for dreamers for without them we would not have most of the useful things we use in life today! Today let us walk by faith and not by sight.

In Jesus mighty name

Amen

Matthew 6:33

33 But seek first his kingdom(A) and his righteousness, and all these things will be given to you as well.

Notes

Notes

Day 6

Good morning, Abba,

As we wake up to a new week we also wake up to a new day, and you indeed make all things new. So let us just lay down all the worries and things that didn't work out last week and walk into this week completely covered in the full armor of God.

Abba this week has many unknowns and we only have our human mind to use as we walk forward, so let us remember you set us on this path and you know everything we face and all the blessings waiting on us as we choose to put you first this day and week.

Abba your simply amazing let us truly walk in the truth and freedom of your favor this week!

In Jesus name

Amen

Lamentations 3:22-23

22 The steadfast love of the Lord never ceases;

     his mercies never come to an end;

23 They are new every morning;

     great is your faithfulness

Notes

Notes

Day 7

Good morning God,

Today we wake up with thanksgiving in our hearts but some unsolved circumstances staring us on the face. We press on towards the goal set before us in faith.

Let us be a light in this crazy dark world today and let us be strong knowing even in our weakness you provide strength as we wait upon you.

God today we lay all our cares upon you and we rest in your loving arms knowing all things work together for the hood of those who love you...

In Jesus mighty name

Amen

Philippians 3:14

14 I press on(A) toward the goal to win the prize(B) for which God has called(C) me heavenward in Christ Jesus

Notes

Notes

Day 8

Good morning, Abba,

Today I want to just thank you for all you do for me. I know so many times we only do this when something huge happens like we get a bonus at work or promotion but I believe we should thank you for it all.

The hard stuff is usually where we grow and that place is where we tend to lean to you that much more. Abba helps us to reach for you on every breath and moment not because we are struggling but because you love us and made us to be in relationship with you.

So today Abba thank you not for a thing but thank you for you!!

In Jesus name we pray

Amen

Ephesians 3:20

Giving thanks always for all things unto God and the Father in the name of our Lord Jesus Christ;

Notes

Notes

Day 9

Dear God,

Stripping is hard, it hurts and it's scary. However, I do know you must strip us of all the layers for us to fully walk in what you have for us.

So today God I say yes, yes to the stripping, yes to the pain and yes to the freedom and abundance on the other side of the stripping.

Lord takes us deep into the holy secret place and build us back up in the way you need us to be. Have your way God

Today let your will be done on earth as it is in heaven!

In Jesus name

Amen

John 15:2

He cuts off every branch in me that bears no fruit, while every branch that does bear fruit, he prunes so that it will be even more fruitful.

Notes

Notes

Day 10

Good morning God,

I just want to thank you. You are so amazing and kind and beautiful. I do so want to also repent for not taking time to say that but even more to repent for not truly understanding my own beauty.

God, you live inside of me thru Holy Spirit and that is a very beautiful core to my life. You also have healed my soul and allowed me to grow so much.

God thank you for not loving me the way I love me but instead for teaching me to love me the way you love me.

Today I just want to be.

I just want to sit and soak in your amazing precious presence.

Thanks God you rock thanks for helping me see me with your eyes.

In Jesus precious name

Amen

3 John 1:2

Beloved, I wish above all things that thou mayest prosper and be in health, even as thy soul prospers

Notes

Notes

Day 11

Dear God,

Today I want to thank you, thank you that you love me so much that you allow things to wake me up in only a way I need.

God thank you for my family even though I have much work to do there as well, I am grateful for each of them and I am allowing you to break my heart for what breaks yours.

I don't know exactly how I got to this point but it's time to stop plowing because sometimes when you plow you don't see the things under the snow or earth that are hidden and you plow over them. God forgive me for plowing over those amazing blessings in my life you call people

I admit plowing became a defense mechanism and I am sure at times protected me but ultimately, it's only you that can protect me. As I let the little girl on me out of the cage last week, I never expected to have such a quick opportunity to choose to trust you.

God, I have dug a pit and it wasn't out of trying to be rich and famous it was out of trying to protect myself and so in my way sometimes, it's so deceptive that the lies I believe I had thought were truth.

Anyway, as I continue to process thru God my prayer for each of us is that we will simply stop. Stand. And listen. The amazing thing about you God is it's never too late and you can redeem anything even our worst mistakes.

So, I stand humbled and open to whatever you need to show me or tell me so I can truly walk in my full purpose your way not mine.

And God send the clean-up angels because man I have left a path of destruction which is exactly opposite of what I wanted to leave. Fix it God, I love you

In Jesus name,

Amen

Romans 8:28

28 And we know that in all things God works for the good of those who love him, who have been called according to his purpose

Notes

Notes

Day 12

Good morning, Lord,

Today I want to thank you for letting us live and giving us so many blessings and I am sorry we don't always recognize those blessings or say thank you.

We do complain and murmur much like the Israelites, so please forgive us Lord. Today as we sit with you show us exactly where we need to let go and where we need to take action.

Lord so many times we run ahead of you and we dig pits instead of wells the we fall in our own pit. Even though we thought we were doing what you wanted us to do sometimes we just run ahead a little too much.

So today I run back and I ask you to show me how to start filling in the pit and how to actually move forward so I don't do those things anymore.

Lord, it looks dark and we have made a mess but I know you can redeem anything so I ask for a miracle for whatever area we need finances, housing, physical healing, or mental turmoil just help us God and heal us as we let go and let God.

Let us seek you first and truly stop chasing anything else because everything else is futile.

I love you and thank you for not treating me like I have treated myself.

In Jesus mighty name

Amen

Isaiah 41:10

So do not fear, for I am with you;

      do not be dismayed, for I am your God.

I will strengthen you and help you;

      I will uphold you) with my righteous right hand

Notes

Notes

Day 13

Dear Abba,

Today I crave a deeper relationship with you. I have settled for surface for so long and you have blessed me but there is more.

I want to be so deep in you I don't see my flesh anymore. I want others to see my transparency as they see you first.

I may not know exactly what that looks like but I am tired of settling for less than you have for me both in relationship and wisdom actually in everything.

I have gotten stuck in a microwave mentality and been so full of myself my favorite phrase is or was "I got it" man to think how many times I thought or said that.

First, I am sorry for just scratching the surface getting some blessings and moving on in my own power. Second please let me know more of you and more of who you created me to be.

Today I ask forgiveness for pride and grace to enter into the more with you not ahead and not behind but right beside you. Let's do this together like I know you have asked me for a long time and I couldn't hear you over my own plans.

I surrender to the call of deeper thank you for your patience and grace.

In Jesus mighty Name

Amen

Psalms 42:7

Deep calls to deep in the roar of your waterfalls; all your waves and breakers have swept over me

Notes

Notes

Day 14

Dear God

Today I lift up families sometimes we get so focused on our own wants and desires we forget to include you. We lash out and want our own way when truly we should stop and ask "what do you want God".

So today I want to know what you want to do with all those amazing pieces to my family puzzle. I spend a lot of time telling you what I would like to see but maybe you could give me your eyes to see how you want it all to look.

Oh, and please forgive my impetuous actions and words. I don't always think before I act or speak where these nations are concerned, I text back what I think is best when in reality you probably have a better way.

So, forgive me Father and show me your heart for these and anyone else who comes into my path.

In Jesus name

I want to love them like you love me

Amen

Psalms 46:10

He says, "Be still, and know that I am God;

     I will be exalted among the nations,

I will be exalted in the earth."

Notes

Notes

Day 15

Good morning, Father,

Today I want to know what are your dreams for me. I have spent my life running after things and people. I have made vision boards and plans and asked you to bless them.

However, I have never stopped to sit with you and dream. Your dream board the Bible shows me so many promises over my life. I know you want to give me my hearts desires.

This week you have shown me it's not just about asking it's about trusting and surrendering with belief. Belief in myself and my worth that if I do ask you anything you will indeed give it to me.

My perspective has shifted a little though because I really want to know what your dreams for me are so today let's chat.

I love you Daddy I can't wait to hear and see what you want for me and then to allow you to bring it to pass what a season this shall be.

Thank you, Daddy, for not smiting me off the planet for being a brat because oh my I have been a big fat Brat but your so loving that you just wait and protect us even from ourselves.

I love you Father,

Thank you and see you soon

Amen

Joel 2:28

"It will come about after this

     That I will pour out My Spirit on all mankind;

And your sons and daughters will prophesy,

     Your old men will dream dreams,

Your young men will see visions.

Notes

Notes

Day 16

Dear Lord,

Today I want to say thank you.

Thank you for loving me when I am unlovable.

Thank you for helping me even when I made the mess.

Thank you for bringing light into dark places thru me and for me.

Thanks for being with me in it all.

Thanks for never leaving me or forsaking me

Thanks for giving me people to grow me and teach me and move me forward in so many areas

But mostly just thank you for loving me with a love so deep and so perfect I don't have to do anything to earn it all I have to do is receive it and pass it along.

Lord let me pay it forward like you do

In your amazing mighty Name

Amen

Deuteronomy 31:8

8 The Lord himself goes before you and will be with you;(A) he will never leave you nor forsake you. (B) Do not be afraid; do not be discouraged

Notes

Notes

Day 17

Dear Abba,

Today I want to pray over my kids and grands. You loaned them to me to raise and love and advise, I am afraid I have messed it up from time to time.

Abba, they have struggled at times and instead of asking you to fix it I went into fixer mode and oh boy did I ever not fix it.

I kept them from their own mess and from seeking you to get out of it. I truly thought that I was doing the right thing but now I see I was simply allowing them the easy way out and actually making it easy on me as well because it hurts to see them struggle.

So, forgive me Abba for stepping in when I should have just prayed for you and them to connect deeper. I will indeed be more cautious about rescuing from this point on.

The most important thing is each of those nations come to know you in a personal level and if they are anything like their momma that may take some struggle.

I love you Abba

In Jesus name

Amen

Proverbs 3:5-6

5 Trust in the Lord with all your heart

and lean not on your own understanding;

6 in all your ways submit to him,

and he will make your paths straight

Notes

Notes

Day 18

Dear Father,

Yesterday we got handed one of those surprise opportunities. I thought I was okay with it then in the night the fear came.

Thank you for helping me settle my mind and spirit and realize my first reaction and advise wasn't correct and even opened a door to fear.

It seems the path I want to take usually goes back to my survival roots and not my trusting you roots. You have helped me with a lot of inner work and I believe last night was a test or opportunity to see if I would rely on me and manipulate to work it out or if I would fully trust you to work in whatever way you want.

I choose You Father all day every day and even if your answer which is in my best interest isn't in the package, I want it to be in.

So, this morning I thank you again, I thank you that all things work for my good and your glory and that no weapon formed against me shall prosper.

I will walk today with a smile of joy and peace knowing my Father has my back and I have His favor in all I do I am blessed!

Love you Father,

In Jesus name

Amen

Isaiah 54:17

17 No weapon formed against you shall (A)prosper,

And every tongue which rises against you in judgment
You shall condemn.

This is the heritage of the servants of the Lord,

(B)And their righteousness is from Me,"

Says the Lord

Notes

Notes

Day 19

Dear Abba,

Good morning, I so thank you for never leaving me or forsaking me. Thank you that even when I wake up in the night you are there ready to combat the lies with truth.

Condemnation is not from you and neither is constant spinning of thoughts on how to fix a circumstance. I am learning that trust has to be a deep thing abs I have had so many trust issues on my life I don't allow you in every single space yet.

Thank you for being patient and showing me the places, I have had so much disappointment in man and hope deferred that I wasn't surrendering those parts to you.

That is one reason I have allowed the enemy to torment me with lies and condemnation because of hadn't fully forgiven myself and trusted you with the outcome. It may not look like I want but I know I can't self-protect or fix anymore.

This is a deep work we are doing God and I am so thankful because even if some things look different you are still a good good father and I am still your daughter and I am enough.

Thank you, Abba, for your patience and grace and favor I love that even when I mess it up you can still make it work out for me!

In Jesus name

I love you Daddy

Amen

Hebrews 13:5

5 Keep your lives free from the love of money(A) and be content with what you have, (B) because God has said,

"Never will I leave you;

never will I forsake you

Notes

Notes

Day 20

Dear God,

Wow what a day yesterday was I enjoyed being me, thank you for helping me peel back the layers and begin to walk more fully in who you designed me to be.

Also thank you for reigning me back in this morning as I almost went off on my own plan without sitting with you first. I am so thankful for the peace and strategies.

It's so easy for us to just rush around doing all the things but a lot of times we miss doing the only thing that matters. Sitting with our God.

God as we embark on this weekend help me to stay in the place of rest and peace and also find joy in every moment because every breath is truly a gift.

God I can't wait to dream with you and hear what your dreams are for me, thanks for the invite and thanks for helping me slow down enough to hear you!

Love you God

Amen

Isaiah 40:31

31 But they that wait upon the Lord shall renew their strength; they shall mount up with wings as eagles; they shall run, and not be weary; and they shall walk, and not faint

Notes

Notes

Day 21

Dear Father,

Today I thank you that you are good all the time and you never change. You are the same yesterday, today and tomorrow.

It's our world and ourselves that our constantly wavering back and forth. God help us to stay steady even in the winds of the world. Help us to truly fix our eyes on you and know that if we do that everything else will fall into place.

So many times, we start strong but when it takes longer than we think or doesn't go how we thought it would, or looks different than we expected we want to throw in the towel.

When in reality your thoughts and ways are so much higher than ours, we probably can't even fathom or imagine what and how you will work it out. Then in comes the enemy of our souls many times out of our own mouth we murmur and complain and block a blessing you simply wanted to give us in your way and timing.

Forgive me God for murmuring and help my unbelief. Help me to hold tight to the one who sends the miracles not the miracle itself. I will hold your garment and receive healing; I will listen to the still small voice and find the path you set before me.

God you're simply amazing and today I say thank you!! I trust you and I believe! I believe in me and You and that is a winning combo!

In Jesus name

Amen

Hebrews 13:8

Jesus Christ the same yesterday, and today, and for ever

Notes

Notes

Day 22

Good morning, Lord,

Today I just want to say thank you. Thank you for my family. Thank you for my home. Just thank you for letting me wake up today and for giving me the ability to get up.

Lord, I know so many times we take everything for granted including you. We wake up with our to do list but just for us but also for the One who created us.

We know exactly what we want you to do for us and although we say we understand you're not a genie in a bottle we treat you exactly like that. We get up every day and make our three wishes and expect it to just happen and when it doesn't, we are angry not at ourselves but at you.

I know this is an easy pattern to fall into because I have been there many times. Life is hard sometimes and that you promised us in the Bible. But so many more times you tell us to trust and not fear.

It seems we cover our fears with anger and frustration and every other emotion out there when what we truly need to do is simply say" God this is what I want but what do you want, how do you want this to work out?"

I am sorry God for I always have the way figured out on my own head and I do get frustrated when it doesn't go that way, please forgive me and help me to trust your ways are truly higher than mine and you indeed work everything out for my good and your glory.

Also help me remember I have the power in my mouth to silence the enemy and also change things many times in those very situations I am praying about.

So today God what is on your heart?

Let's do that!

In Jesus name

Amen

Isaiah 55:9

9 "As the heavens are higher than the earth,

so are my ways higher than your ways

and my thoughts than your thoughts

Notes

Notes

Day 23

Dear Abba

Okay yesterday was a whirlwind and the only way I made it thru that storm was to hold tight to your promises.

I was blindsided by the way it came in but so thankful that nothing takes you by surprise abba.

I am still not 💯 sure what we are to do but I am a 💯 sure you are the answer to all things. Yes, we tend to create messes that we don't really mean to or understand even how sometimes it comes to this point. We think if we fight with faith we will win and we will in heaven but earthside man that's a whole different ballgame.

You never leave me or forsake me and your ways are higher than mine but sometimes I would love to know how things will work out the way you already do.

So today Abba just holds me, just don't let go this storm has been brewing for years and it's coming to the end of the cycle and season. That is a great thing but man riding the waves is proving to be a big deal and a bit more intense than I thought it would.

Thanks for inside information from Holy Spirit and a strategy to pray and steps to take on the natural. I trust you God and I believe in both of us. I know you created me for a time such as this so let's do this.

The final countdown is here after this it all opens up one last traffic jam and then we got a clearer road and thank you for teaching us how not to go around this mountain again!

I love you Abba thanks for being my friend and protector and guide thru the storms.

In Jesus name

Amen

John 14:6

6 Jesus answered, "I am the way and the truth and the life. No one comes to the father except through me

Notes

Notes

Day 24

Dear God

Today I am grateful to wake up but if I am honest, I am a bit sad and disappointed.

It seems what I have been standing for six years and hard cord for the last two is unraveling in front of my eyes. I have stood on the verse you told me too thru prayer but it isn't happening exactly like what I heard, at least not yet.

I know I have to walk by faith and not by sight and I know it's not over until you say it's over. But my flesh side is tired, sad and a bit disillusioned with the situation.

But you know my heart and I am grateful I can spill all this out and talk with you about it because otherwise it sits in my soul and rots.

So today I choose to let all the disappointments and confusion go, I choose to believe you are working it all

Out for my good and your glory and I continue to stand that you are providing all my needs thru your riches and glory in Christ Jesus.

I also choose to ignore and bind the enemy if at any point he brings his slimy tail in my direction, I will not entertain any thoughts but God thoughts I will capture every thought and make it obedient to that of the mind of Christ.

I love you God and even if it's a different way your still good and I still trust you and fully surrender to your way.

In Jesus name

Amen

Isaiah 43:18-19

Notes

Notes

Day 25

Good morning, Abba

What a week, I have been so grateful to you for every single moment even the hard ones.

I am honored to have the privilege to walk this thing called life out hand in hand with you. I truly am seeing the Word in action as I trust in you and not my own understanding.

Abba, please continue to heal those places in me that have been hidden for years because I want to be pure so that I can shine your light to the nations.

I woke up today for the first time in six years without fear or dread. It's a process but I am excited to see what comes next. Also, this week I have dealt with the fact that I am walking out my faith not just speaking it.

So, with a busy day and weekend ahead I just want to say thank you for it all, thank you for the fire that as it burns hotter it removes more impurities and as I allow you the potter to do the shaping, I am becoming more of who you created me to be.

Peel more layers and have your way God because in you I fully trust and surrender to the process. It's not easy but I am

Worth it!

In Jesus name

Amen

Jeremiah 33:3

3 'Call to me and I will answer you and tell you great and unsearchable things you do not know.'

Notes

Notes

Day 26

Dear Lord,

Thank you for a very nice weekend weather wise and also for us to spend time together. Thank you for allowing us to have a few calls and not be stacked busy. I realize that we are in a manna season and a bit of a valley.

That doesn't mean that we did anything wrong necessarily but that we need some more time to grow and get closer to you. You are such a good Father that you will not send us to the promised land unprepared because we would indeed squander the spoils.

Although the valleys are not my favorite place to be I have come to accept and appreciate I need them. It's so easy on the mountain top to lose track of who got me there. But in the valley, it's easy to stay close and now I fully see no matter where I am on the journey it's that secret space of dwelling with you that matters.

Everything else is really meaningless, I mean living in the earth realm means that we need provision and it's super nice to have extra but sometimes I have to go back to square one and just be grateful for the manna.

I guess I am more like the Israelites than I like to admit. So maybe this is the last time I am in the wilderness before the promised land is released to me and I am gleaning all I can so that when I cross over for that final time, I am prepared to steward it well.

So many things are gifts and we miss it many times complaining about the very situations that lead to breakthrough. So, thank you for the valleys and thank you for the peaks, thank you for the manna and thank you for the abundance in all things I will give thanks and be content!

Ps- I really am ready for the mountain top again just saying!

In Jesus name

Amen

Psalms 23:4

Even though I walk

      through the darkest valley,

I will fear no evil,

      for you are with me;

your rod and your staff,

      they comfort me

Notes

Notes

Day 27

Good morning God,

Thank you for waking us up today. Thank you for every single blessing we have and thank you for helping us to see each moment is a true blessing. Let us count our blessings and give thanks for each one. All good gifts come from a good Father who likes to bless us.

Forgive us for those moments we lose sight of this fact, forgive us for grumbling and complaining as the Israelites did in the wilderness. We repent for our short-sighted doubting hearts.

Lord today let us see that we are truly blessed let us bless someone else and always we give thanks for your breath in our lungs. We appreciate and honor you lord we are humbled to be vessels that you use on the earth please help us to be the best us and who you made us to be in your mighty sons name we pray

Amen

Matthew 5:8

8. Blessed are the pure in heart,

> for they will see God

Notes

Notes

Day 28

Father God,

I come to you this morning bringing everything illness, infirmity or injury before your throne of mercy and grace. I lift it all up to you, your word says by your stripes we are healed so today Lord I claim this healing on behalf of anyone who is struggling or not whole.

Lord, we repent for any sin known or unknown that could have allowed the enemy a foothold in our body's minds or souls. We want to prosper like our souls prosper but first we must be shalom whole and forgiven to do this. That wholeness can't come from any other source but you.

So, Father we receive forgiveness and healing and we will stand and walk in the promise for now and evermore. We won't turn back but instead keep our eyes focused at all times on you and watch as all things are added into our lives. Thank you, Father, for the answer!!!

In Jesus name we pray.

Amen

Ephesians 6:13

13 Therefore put on the full armor of God, (A)so that when the day of evil comes, you may be able to stand your ground, and after you have done everything, to stand

Notes

Notes

Day 29

Abba,

Today I lift up everyone who had pushed their body to the limit. I ask that you show us how to truly operate in rest while working as unto you.

We tend to push so hard striving to hit goals when sometimes the true goal is simply being still and allowing you to fight and or work on our behalf.

Abba you are such a good Father, you give us opportunity to see that we are not able to do what you can do neither can we see what you can see. Today I pray for peace and patience in the storm.

Abba, we love you and we fully surrender to your plan for us because it is better than anything we could ask for dream of or imagine.

In Jesus name

Amen

Hebrews 4: 9-11

9 There remains, then, a Sabbath-rest for the people of God; 10 for anyone who enters God's rest also rests from their works, just as God did from his. 11 Let us, therefore, make every effort to enter that rest, so that no one will perish by following their example of disobedience

Notes

Notes

Day 30

Father,

I pray this morning for clarity. I ask for all of us who are walking thru what seems to be a fog.

Give us ultimate clarity and peace of mind on which path to take. Let us not take it in our own hands and run ahead of your word or angels but instead let us stand on faith realizing what you close is supposed to be closed and yet another open door will be sent, you know our needs just as you take care of the birds of the air, they have all their needs provided for and yet do not work or toil for it.

Father, let us have peace that surpasses understanding and as we begin a new year of 5783 let us stand upon your promises and walk in the faith and love to see it all come to pass with ease and flow in Jesus mighty name

Amen

Philippians 4:7

7 And the peace of God, which surpasses all understanding, will guard your hearts and your minds in Christ Jesus

Notes

Notes

About the Author

Dawn Hill is a wife to an amazing man named Scott, they have been married for over 30 years. They have raised 4 amazing kids and now have 7 amazing grandchildren to share life with and enjoy. Dawn's heart is to see everyone live their best life and truly run after their God given Destiny. She believes prayer is vital in this process. She coaches others on how to take their life to the next level as well.

To contact Dawn or book her for your next event reach out anytime to:

Dawn Hill

Levelupwithdawn@gmail.com

Fb- @DawnHill

IG- @faithvoyager

Thank you for investing in your life and the lives of others thru prayer!

Stay tuned for the next prayer book release in spring 2023!

Made in the USA
Columbia, SC
15 February 2023

12075945R00057